Contents

David Beckham.

1 Childhood

David Robert Joseph Beckham was born
in London on 2 May 1975.
He grew up in Leytonstone,
in the East End.

He went to Chase Lane Juniors
and Chingford High School.
David Beckham was never very good at
school-work.
He just wanted to be a footballer.

The nearest big clubs to David Beckham
were Spurs and West Ham.
But David Beckham's dad
supported Manchester United.
So did David Beckham.
He wanted to play for Manchester United.
He wanted to play at Old Trafford.
He was crazy about Manchester United.
David Beckham's hero was Manchester United
captain Bryan Robson.
He used to watch Manchester United when they
played in London.
When Manchester United played at West Ham,
David Beckham was the Manchester United mascot!

When David Beckham was eight he played for
Ridgeway Rovers.
They were good. They once won 23–0!
He also played for Waltham Forest and
for Essex schoolboys.
The local paper called him
the 'Chingford football sensation'.

When David Beckham was 11
he entered a competition.
It was run by Bobby Charlton's Coaching School.
Kids from all over the country took part.
To win you needed good ball control.
David Beckham reached the final.
Guess where it was? Old Trafford!

Bobby Charlton was amazed.
David Beckham was the best 11-year-old
he had ever seen.
David Beckham won the competition.
The prize was a two week holiday in Spain,
at the Nou Camp stadium in Barcelona.
There he met Gary Lineker,
Mark Hughes and Terry Venables.

2 Signing On

London clubs soon heard about the boy wonder.
He had trials with Spurs and Leyton Orient.
Spurs wanted to sign him.
But David Beckham only wanted to play
for Manchester United.

One day he was playing for Waltham Forest.
A scout from Manchester United saw the game.
United asked him for a trial.
They liked what they saw.
On 2 May 1991, Alex Ferguson
signed him for United.
It was David Beckham's sixteenth birthday.

David Beckham amazes people with his skills.

3 Old Trafford

United had some very famous players
and had just won the Cup-Winners' Cup.
Alex Ferguson wanted to win the Championship.
He was planning for the future.
He had some brilliant young players.
They spent all their time practising.

No one had heard of them in those days.
They have now:
  Paul Scholes,
  Gary Neville,
  Phil Neville,
  Nicky Butt,
  Robbie Savage,
  Keith Gillespie and
  David Beckham.

In 1992, United's Youth team won
the FA Youth Cup.
David Beckham scored in the final.

4 First Team Football

In October 1992, David Beckham played
in the first team.
He came on as a substitute against Brighton
in the League Cup. He was just 17.

The next season he did not play for
the first team at all – just for the Reserves.
That season Manchester United
won the Reserves' League.

Alex Ferguson wanted to give
his young players first team football.
David Beckham went on loan to Preston North
End. He played only four games for Preston
but he scored twice.
He was Man of the Match three times.

David Beckham didn't play a full game for United
until April 1995.
It was against Leeds, at Old Trafford.

5 Number 7

David Beckham was soon a regular in the
first team.
He played right midfield and
scored eight goals in his first full season.

He scored against Chelsea
in the FA Cup semi-final.
In the Cup final
Cantona scored the winning goal
from a Beckham cross.
That season Manchester United won the Double.
(This means they won the League and the Cup.)

The next season United were Champions again.
David Beckham scored 12 goals.
He scored his most famous goal
against Wimbledon.
The Wimbledon keeper was off his line.
David Beckham tried a shot from the half-way line.
It went in!

Celebrating David Beckham's famous goal against Wimbledon.

He scored another amazing goal against Chelsea.
He hit the ball so hard
it went in at about 160 kilometres per hour.
David Beckham was voted Young Player of the Year.

At the end of the season Eric Cantona retired.
Who was going to wear his Number 7 shirt?
David Beckham.
Just like his hero Bryan Robson,
he wore it for the Charity Shield match.
By mistake, his name was spelt BECKAM
on the shirt!
That season he scored 11 goals
and he only missed one League game.

6 Europe

Alex Ferguson had won everything
except the Champions' League.

Manchester United reached the quarter-finals.
They reached the semi-finals –
but they could not get any further.
In 1997, they reached the semi-finals again
but were knocked out.

In 1998–1999 it was different.
Manchester United beat LKS Lodz.
They put 11 goals past Brondby.
David Beckham scored.
They drew with Barcelona.
David Beckham scored.
They drew with Bayern Munich.

United beat Inter Milan in the quarter-final.
Dwight Yorke scored twice from Beckham's crosses.

They beat Juventus in the semi-final.
Roy Keane scored from a Beckham corner.

They met Bayern Munich again in the final.
The game was at the Nou Camp in Barcelona.
About 90,000 people saw the game live.
Millions watched it on TV.

Bayern Munich were winning 1–0.
The game went into injury time.
Then Teddy Sheringham equalised.
Bayern Munich could not believe it.
Two minutes later Manchester United scored again.

Man United were European Champions!

7 Champions

That season, Beckham also helped
United win the FA Cup.
His goal against Spurs
brought the championship back to Old Trafford.
United was the first English club
to win the Treble.
(This means they won the League, the FA Cup and
the Champions' League in the same season.)
They were the champions again in 2000,
and again in 2001.

David Beckham played 388 times for United.
He scored a total of 86 goals for them.
He created a lot more goals with his
fantastic crosses, corners and free-kicks.
And he never stopped running.
He ran an average of 14.5 kilometres every game.
But he got hurt a lot.
He was fouled more times
than the other United players.
He wore a new pair of boots every game.
They cost £300 each.

In 2001, all the top managers and players in FIFA
voted David Beckham the second best footballer
in the whole world.
He was second only to the great Luis Figo.

8 England

In 1996, England manager Glen Hoddle
picked David for England.
No one outside England had heard
of David Beckham.
But that soon changed.

In the 1998 World Cup,
he took a free-kick against Columbia.
He curled the ball around the wall.
It beat the Columbian keeper.
GOAL! England won 2–0.
Beckham was a national hero!

In the next round, England played Argentina.
England were leading 2–1.
Then David Beckham was fouled.
He retaliated.
The referee saw it
and brought out a red card.

Beckham is shown the red card.

David Beckham had never been sent off before.
Argentina soon scored again.
England were knocked out on penalties.

Some fans were angry with David Beckham.
But he carried on playing for England.
In November 2000, he was made England captain.
He led England to a 5–1 victory over Germany.

In October 2001, England played Greece
at Old Trafford.
England had to draw to reach
the World Cup finals.
Greece scored first.
But David Beckham never stopped running.
He was everywhere.
He was brilliant.
He took an amazing free-kick,
and Teddy Sheringham back-headed it
into the goal.
Greece scored again.
Beckham hit the side-netting.
Time was running out.
Then, in the last seconds,
England were given a free-kick.

It was 25 yards (23 metres) out.
It was the last kick of the game.
David Beckham went to take it.
Could he do it?
He bent it around the wall
and into the net.
GOAL!!!

Just before the 2002 World Cup,
David Beckham broke a bone in his foot.
Every England fan was worried
he would miss the World Cup.
But he was ready in time
to play against Argentina.
England were given a penalty.
Beckham went to take it.
The Argentina players tried to put him off.
They tried to remind him about
that red card.
But Beckham was determined.
He sent the keeper the wrong way.
GOAL!

David Beckham led England into the quarter-finals.
But they were knocked out by Brazil.

In the run-up to Euro 2004,
David Beckham scored five goals in seven games.
In the first group game against France
he set up a cross for Frank Lampard.
This put England ahead.
Then England were given a penalty.
David Beckham stepped up to take it.
But Fabien Barthez saved it.

David Beckham led England into
the quarter-finals again.
At the end of a fantastic game with Portugal
the score was a 2–2 draw.
It went to penalties.
David Beckham took the first penalty.
But he slipped and hit the ball over the bar.
England went out 5–6 on penalties.

In eight years, David Beckham
has won 75 England caps.
He has been a fantastic captain of his country.

Can he lead England
to win the World Cup in 2006?

9 Real Madrid

In the summer of 2003,
David Beckham left Old Trafford.
He moved to Spanish champions
Real Madrid for £25 million.
He is now a 'galactico'
like Ronaldo, Zidane and Figo.
This means he is so good
he must be from another planet!

When he signed for Real Madrid,
the club started selling shirts with his name on.
They sold out on the first day!

David Beckham soon settled into Spanish football.
He scored five goals in his first 16 games.
He played 47 games in his first season in Spain
and scored seven goals.
He helped Real Madrid reach the quarter-finals
of the Champions' League
and win the Spanish Super Cup.

David Beckham with some of his Real Madrid team-mates.

10 Fame

In 1997, David Beckham met Victoria Adams.
She was one of the Spice Girls.
She was known as Posh Spice.
Guess where they first met. Old Trafford!

It was love at first sight.
They tried to keep it a secret.
But the press soon found out.

Newspapers and TV follow them everywhere.
Sometimes they enjoy their fame.
Sometimes they want to be left alone.

He bought her a necklace worth £25,000.
Her name is tattooed on his left arm.

In July 1999, Victoria and David got married.
The wedding was held at a castle in Ireland.
There was a firework display
and an orchestra playing Spice Girls hits.

The Spice Girls were at the wedding.

All the United players were there.

Gary Neville was the best man.

Even the priest wore Manchester United socks!

David and Victoria now have two sons,

called Brooklyn and Romeo.

Their names are tattooed on David's body too.

It was love at first sight for David and Victoria.

11 Fortune

David and Victoria own two houses.
One is in Spain and
the other is near London.
The one near London is called 'Beckingham Palace'.
David owns seven cars,
including a Ferrari,
a Porsche, an Aston Martin
and a bullet-proof Mercedes.
He advertises sports-wear, drinks,
biscuits, engine oil and sunglasses.
He models clothes.
He even has his own designer label.
He has been voted 'the world's sexiest man'.

His favourite food is sticky toffee pudding
and butterscotch sauce.
He likes hip-hop music,
especially Dr Dre, Jay-Z and P Diddy.
He has been a DJ in a London nightclub.

David has made a lot of money from advertising things from
engine oil to designer clothes.

Every time David changes his haircut,
thousands of fans copy him.
There is a film named after him,
Bend It Like Beckham.
There is even a sausage named after him,
called the World Cup Bender!

David Beckham plays for
the biggest football club in the world.
He is captain of England.
He scores amazing goals.
He is the best crosser in the game.
He is handsome, talented,
famous, lucky, successful
and very, very rich.
And he is still so young.

Key Dates

1975	David Beckham born
1986	Wins football competition and holiday to Spain
1991	Signs for Manchester United
1992	Scores in FA Youth Cup Final
1992	Plays in Manchester United first team
1995	Plays first full game for Manchester United
1996	Helps Manchester United win the Double
1997	Manchester United win the League
1997	Voted Young Player of the Year
1998	Sent off against Argentina in the World Cup
1999	Marries Victoria Adams
1999	Helps Manchester United win the Treble

2000	Becomes England captain
2000	Helps Manchester United win the League
2001	Helps Manchester United win the League
2001	Scores against Greece to take England to the World Cup finals
2003	Helps Manchester United win the League
2003	Awarded OBE
2003	Moves to Real Madrid for £25 million